ARCHITECTURE & DESIGN LIBRARY

MODERN STYLE

Elinor Friedman Felcher

FRIEDMAN/FAIRFAX
PUBLISHERS

A FRIEDMAN/FAIRFAX BOOK

© 1998 by Michael Friedman Publishing Group, Inc.

Library of Congress Cataloging-in-Publication Data available upon request.

ISBN 1-56799-547-0

Editors: Francine Hornberger and Sharyn Rosart
Art Director: Jeff Batzli
Layout Design: Jennifer Markson
Photography Editor: Wendy Missan
Production Manager: Camille Lee

Color separations by Colourscan Overseas Co Pte Ltd
Printed and bound in China by Leefung-Asco Printers Ltd

1   3   5   7   9   10   8   6   4   2

For bulk purchases and special sales, please contact:
Friedman/Fairfax Publishers
Attention: Sales Department
15 West 26th Street
New York, New York 10010
212/685-6610   FAX 212/685-1307

Visit our website:
http://www.metrobooks.com

Special thanks to Jean Hines, Librarian at the New York School of Interior Design, for directing me to sources within the library and for guarding my volumes from reshelving; to the Cooper-Hewitt Museum library staff for their help and cooperation; and to Martin for his love and support and patience with late-night typing

Contents

INTRODUCTION

W hat is modern style? It is usually thought of as simple and minimal. In a word, less. But styles evolve. Definitions vary. Some might call it less cluttered, more pure. Less flamboyant, more restrained. Less ornamental, simpler. Less eccentric, more utilitarian. While many in the design field embrace modern style design, there are many different degrees of this concept. But underlying them all is a yearning for more practical solutions to everyday needs. Modern style helps our homes to be a better fit. Our furnishings become more streamlined, more functional, and ultimately, more liberating, balancing the psychological and physical demands of our lives.

Modernism actually has its roots in the 1890s, when a radical departure in design began with a movement called the Vienna Secession. Led by Otto Wagner (1841–1918), a revered Austrian architect, a group of successful fellow architects turned away from the historic, elegant, ornamental design they had once embraced and began to experiment with straight lines and simple, practical solutions for space and furnishings, shocking many in their professional community.

Their desire to change was influenced by the political and industrial environment of the late nineteenth century. The seeds of the modernist movement can be seen in this startling transition.

Early in the twentieth century in Italy, Holland, and Germany cells of artists and architects continued to experiment with antiestablishment design. The Bauhaus movement in Germany grew out of some of these new ideas. After World War I many artists and architects were excited by the promise of the machine age, of the possibilities inherent in the mass production of economical, straight-lined furniture. They wanted to be free of the restrictions placed on the specialized furnishings of the past, when furniture was designed for a particular room, and a bedroom chair could never be placed in the living room.

OPPOSITE: *Having a modern style interior does not mean resorting to using only white. In this spacious yet spare dining room, walls papered in a colorful primary hue and gold stripe pattern are accented by a teal wainscot and a painted red ceiling. No accessories are needed, as the wall treatment introduces just enough excitement to the space.*

The Bauhaus, an intellectual commune founded by Walter Gropius (1883–1969) in Weimar, Germany, in 1919, was created to give artists a place where they could freely pursue the development of new design ideas, realized through technology, without the interference of criticism from those who wanted to keep design as it was. The thrust of the new design was that function should determine form. Both Marcel Breuer (1902–1981) and Ludwig Mies van der Rohe (1886–1969) were part of this group.

Bauhaus buildings were clean-lined, geometric structures with white walls and simple furnishings. Glass became an important design material as windows were enlarged and skylights came into use. Sun-filled rooms and enlarged vistas brought the feeling of being closer to nature. Architects and designers strove to produce designs that represented purity and truth, rather than obscuring the basic functions of an object with ornamental distraction.

With Germany on the brink of World War II, the leading members of the Bauhaus left their country and came to North America. Embraced by a tiny modern design movement, members of which inspired the founders of the Museum of Modern Art in New York City, these leading European architects and designers exerted a powerful influence on sophisticated design for the next thirty years and into the present. Schooled in the "International Style" of the masters from the Bauhaus, American architects built with glass, steel, and concrete. Light and space were paramount. Designers crafted furniture of tubular chrome, cane or leather, and bentwood. Well-known examples are the Barcelona Chair by Mies van der Rohe and the Wassily Chair and Cesca Chair by Breuer. The Bauhaus masters brought pure modern design to North America, but their functionalism was ideological, strict. There was no room for free form or competing creative ideas.

In the American Midwest, genius and design innovator Frank Lloyd Wright (1867–1959) followed his own muse. Wright was imbued with a love of nature. He designed homes with windows and roof openings to allow sunlight in and to embrace garden vistas. The landscape and plantings around his homes were critical to the total environment. Looking to the Arts and Crafts movement, Wright used wood and other natural materials for furniture. Under his tutelage, Wright's atelier created furniture, lighting, textiles, and glass design, all to maintain the harmony of the interior with the natural exterior. While Wright's designs were more ornamental than those of the Bauhaus masters, he was instinctively modern. He said it best when he said, "Rooms should be...backgrounds for the life within their walls....And no junk!"

After World War II, North American society experienced a rapid change, economically and socially. Some designers saw this as an opportunity to fashion unusual, exciting furnishings and buildings for an enthusiastic population, but they had difficulty breaking free from the dictates of the revered functionalism. Help came in the form of new designs from Italy in the 1960s: colorful designs in storage (the lightweight, rolling plastic cube); the beanbag chair (unstructured, easily movable); and sofas created from attachable-detachable upholstered sections, to name a few. Flexibility and convenience were beginning to enter the American design vocabulary.

The economic crunch of the 1970s was reflected in art and design: true to its modernist heritage, the movement known as minimalism called for sober, even somber environments employing industrial materials, in the colors of machine culture, most notably metallic

OPPOSITE: *In this strongly modern home, stone is the material of choice for the floor, staircase, the unadorned fireplace, shelving, and an end table—part of which can be seen near the stool. Spare furnishings allow the room's architectural elements, including the staircase, the shelving niche, the long and narrow window, and the simple, striking fireplace to make the statement.*

grays. (Two of the basic elements of minimalism, repetition and grid shapes, translated into mellower natural materials, have become graceful staples of modern style.)

The most influential encouragement to break with strict functionalism came from Robert Venturi, a leading architect, who in his insightful and intellectual essays wrote of the need to move away from the excessively rational, to break the rules, to respond to the needs of contemporary living.

Freed from the strictures of functionalism by the writings of Venturi and other respected members of the design community, designers in the late 1960s, 1970s, and 1980s explored all kinds of ideas, using new materials, new shapes, new colors, and over time, new absurdities—leading some designers to begin the movement toward today's modern style.

Today's renewed interest in modern style really emerged as a reaction to the excesses in design that characterized the late 1970s and 1980s, which were in themselves a rebellion against the functional design first heralded in the 1930s, and popular into the late 1960s. It was a time of prosperity, and many leading architects and designers—and their clients—could afford to break free from the dictates of functional design. Stimulated by a new generation of impulsive, individualistic

OPPOSITE: *Although usually notorious for being havens of personal clutter, bedrooms can easily be designed for openness and order. The built-in unit that surrounds the bed is a clever repository for cherished effects. Whether these effects are hidden behind etched-glass doors, or in plain view on lighted wood shelves, the unit proves to be both functional and beautiful. The foot of the bed serves a subtle multipurpose function: footboard and slender table.*

thinkers, and freed by the seemingly unlimited affluence of the 1980s, designers stretched their minds to create furniture and furnishings that would be unique enough to capture attention. Many of the designs were meant to be high-fashion, disposable, and amusing. But in their excitement, many brushed aside the basic tenet of design: serious design must consider function.

During the 1980s, excesses were evident in the scale of homes and in the wit rather than the purpose that drove furniture design. Among the most notable examples of the latter was Memphis, the name chosen for a group of laminate-surfaced furniture pieces decorated with colorful, humorous, and often meaningless designs, produced by a group of leading Italian designers, notable among them Ettore Sottsass. Another style, known as post-modern, exemplified by the work of Michael Graves, presented furniture that was designed with classical architectural details, but was machine-molded and painted in pastel and metallic colors. And not long after, Philippe Starck presented his amusing, provocative, antifunctional designs.

What seemed good at first ultimately began to have a negative impact. Some thoughtful members of the design community were dismayed by what they called a joke for the rich. In the frenzied chase for affluence, some furniture was produced in rare woods or upholstered with precious skins, offending many by the careless use of nonrenewable resources.

By the late 1980s, some designers began to talk of freeing homes from an excess of possessions, of sweeping out the clutter, the overbuying that comes with quick affluence. They argued the overindulgence was distracting, that people were losing perspective, getting out of touch with meaningful values. They encouraged a simpler, more tranquil home environment; surroundings that kept in touch with nature; a home that addressed everyday needs. They saw excess as a distortion, interfering with the ability to contemplate, to reflect, to be in touch with more important issues. Thus began a move toward a redefinition of modern style for the millennium.

The renewed focus on nature required more than using natural materials, it meant using nature itself. Designers' plans for homes featured enlarged windows and doors to provide vistas of nature and to flood rooms with natural light. The beauty of nature would reorder priorities. Furniture would serve function. Accessories would create mood. One of the earliest proponents of the new style, John Pawson, a British designer and architect, wrote that minimalist living offered a sense of liberation, but that this liberation wasn't possible if one was distracted by the trivial.

While some designers pursued the new modernism in its purest form, others wondered how one could really live in such a home. There was greater agreement that design should be spare but not spartan.

Many designers began to be inspired by the new movement's potential for beauty and sought to pioneer a new kind of furniture—innovative, multifunctional pieces that allowed people to live with less. A group of young designers was invited by a group of manufacturers in Italy to create prototypes and soon the marketplace began to offer some interesting ideas often inspired by design ideas of the past, but in a perfectly contemporary translation: furniture that could be easily assembled and disassembled; furniture on wheels for increasingly mobile families; dual-function furniture (chairs with backs that folded down to become tables and coffee tables that could be raised to dining height); space-saving, stylish furniture easily enlarged and easily folded down for small homes (jigsaw-puzzle-cut tables that fit together to form a larger surface) as well as sculptural storage pieces that were useful, and also functioned as art pieces (humorous designs for hatracks and coatracks); provocative accessories; and lower energy art lighting. These "new" minimalists encouraged elegant, playful, technically refined, more affordable design.

Artists began to search for ways to create elements of design using natural and recycled materials. One result was a wall tile made with marble dust and mussel shells; another tile, a floor tile, was made from newspaper and carpet fibers. Designs for lighting from recycled metal and freestanding panels were made from recycled wood. Recycled marble, newspapers, glass, plastic, wallboard, wood pallets, concrete, even garbage have become some of the ingredients for furniture for a new age. Today, design shows, furniture expositions, and lighting fairs exhibit growing numbers of functional and energy-saving designs.

By the mid-1990s, minimalism had begun to recapture popular attention. People yearned to simplify their lives. Frivolous design began to fall out of favor. Modern style, the "new" minimalism, embraces the spirit and ideals of early minimalism, but is warmer, softer, more inviting. Rooms are transformed from stark and sterile to family-friendly havens where solutions have been invented to contain clutter and keep a simple design scheme intact. Less extreme and more environmentally conscious, the new minimalism also embraces color, with neutral palettes and occasional bold flashes of color for emphasis. In a postmodern twist, pieces both old and new are mixed together, making the style both timeless and adaptable.

In the pages that follow, you will find numerous examples of modern, minimal rooms that are both functional and friendly. Less rigid than in its earlier incarnation, today's modern style allows for individual creativity and expression within a harmonious functional context, just right for the spiritual and aesthetic refreshment our fast-paced modern lifestyles require.

OPPOSITE: *A visually arresting gridlike stainless-steel structure serves as a staircase in this relatively bare—but not austere—space. Cleverly playing on an antique theme, the tall yellow-backed chair to the right is actually a chair-table, a furnishing that combines two functions.*

LEFT: *Rich, dark woods give this room a sense of unity from ceiling to window wall to furniture. A variety of textures gives it style. The minimalist cement walls and floor gain warmth when used in combination with the wood; the floors are further warmed with a sisal rug. A copper fireplace becomes the focal point, as it shines in contrast to textures of wood and cement.*

CHAPTER ONE

PRINCIPLES OF MODERN STYLE: NATURE, LIGHT, SIMPLICITY

Modern style seeks to integrate homes into their environments, and thus designs with nature in mind. One of the basic tenets of the movement always has been to bring nature indoors. The easiest way to do this in an existing home is to add or enlarge windows, not only in rooms, but in entrance halls and corridors as well. Walls may be opened to accommodate doors to gardens or patios. Installing skylights opens up views of the natural world, while full walls of glass truly make nature part of the decor. Not surprisingly, picture windows, rather than panes with mullions, are more in keeping with the philosophy of modern style, as they connect the inside to the vista outside without distractions. Rather than add art or objects, modern style might use an unusually shaped window to bring life to an otherwise commonplace wall.

The result of opening up a dwelling with windows is a home flooded with light—another basic design element important in modern style. To make the most of natural light, exterior and interior walls are often painted white or a light, neutral color. Where windows cannot be added easily, artful design can employ artificial light sources to achieve the effect of sunlight. Light may be filtered or tinted to create interesting effects.

With nature and light playing starring roles in the decor, only the simplest furnishings are needed. A sense of open, uncluttered space creates serenity. An absence of distractions allows the room's inhabitants to take pleasure in the pared-down beauty of form and to appreciate the materials that have been used.

The single essential element to making all this work is storage. Without ample, practical storage, it is just not possible to achieve the modern, minimal look. As a result, built-in storage units are ubiquitous in modern style interiors, providing architectural interest as well as places to keep the necessities of life.

OPPOSITE: *Wood and glass doors open to both the balcony and the patio below: easy access to the out-of-doors expands this home's design. The living room flows easily into an outdoor seating area. The stone entry path runs unblocked through the arch to the interior. The shrubbery provides privacy and a connection to nature, emphasized by the stark white walls. The views, the light, and the beauty of the natural materials eliminate the need for excess furnishings or accessories.*

ABOVE: *The walls are painted the color of light, blurring the distinction between inside and out, just as the furnishings dissolve the boundaries between furniture and art in this modern style space.*

OPPOSITE: *The "bones" of this elegant house are set off by the lighting from within. Minimalist frame doors and large terrace windows allow for an unencumbered view outward. The terrace enables easy lounging in full view of nature and provides a roof for the loggia for dining al fresco. The stark white walls magnify the brightness of the sun during the day, while at night, artificial light is reflected off the stone patio and pool.*

LEFT: *Minimalism goes modern, with warm earth shades muting the repetitive motif of vertical windows. The witty, post-modern accent of distressed pool-blue chairs is juxtaposed to the blue urn that acts as a dramatic focal point against the house's rear facade.*

OPPOSITE: *Modern style is often influenced by Zen philosophy, and this serene yard is a fine example. The long, narrow pool is both a sculptural jewel and a delightful amenity. Its stone surround is softened by bamboo plantings. A continuous flow of water from a trough into the pool provides both visual and aural pleasure. Here, the simple flat roof structure with a completely open vista provides an architectural setting in touch with nature.*

ABOVE: *Looking at this simple structure, one's eye is naturally drawn to the artfully designed chimney and niche front door. Four small windows forming a square add an aesthetic statement to an otherwise ordinary wall. Bougainvillea contrast elegantly with the stark white walls and offer a close-up of nature from the patio with its slanted, skylight openings.*

ABOVE: *Utterly simple, the decorative aspects of this deck—the natural wood furniture bleached by the sun, plants in containers, a natural fabric stretched over rafters—allow one to feel immediately in harmony with the environment. Nothing else is required to embellish this natural beauty.*

ABOVE: *According to minimalist theory, contact with nature helps maintain perspective and keeps priorities in order. In this home, doors that open onto a patio offer a sense of freedom and liberation to the home environment. They create a physical connection to the environment, a feeling of wholeness. Shades or curtains would introduce a barrier and thus ruin the effect.*

ABOVE: *A shelving unit made of poles and planks divides the living room and dining room in this interesting space without entirely closing one off from the other. Light pine and various shades of blue create a sense of serenity.*

OPPOSITE: *Sliding glass doors on two sides of this living room give the space the feel of an inviting sun-porch. Soft white furnishings add to the casual comfort. The coral-toned marble floor and wall evoke the beach outside.*

ABOVE: *This entry is reduced to its basics—light, stone, wood, and color. The focus is on entering. Nothing distracts from that. The light reflects on the various natural surfaces, emphasizing the natural materials. The beauty of the elements and the pleasurable simplicity of the entry express the essence of modern style.*

LEFT: *This casual room is a modern style example of the dramatic design possibilities of nature itself—seen through a ten-foot glass wall. A picture window on the side of the room and a clerestory window above the window wall help to amplify the view. A modest collection of natural-material design elements—wood sculpture and rattan furniture as well as baskets seen in the far room—reinforce the idea of nature in use. The uncluttered rooms enable one to enjoy the selected items for their own beauty.*

ABOVE: *This huge expanse of glass without moldings draws the world outside right into the home. The staircase itself, striking in its design, is at once functional and beautiful. No other decorative element is needed in the space. A freestanding sculpture that echoes the stairway design reinforces the purity and tranquility of this home.*

ABOVE: *The pattern of sunlight falling through slats in the ceiling onto textured stone walls; the small windowlike openings in the staircase wall; the wood-framed glass doors showcasing sun-dappled leaves outside; the flush of rose color spilling on the lighted upper wall; and the stone staircase leading to an upper level: all of these elements are emphasized because this entry is not diluted with "things."*

ABOVE: *In a modern environment where furnishings are pared down, the geometry of this exquisite maple staircase with stainless-steel railing and glass guard serves function and art. The floating design can only be successful in an uncluttered space where nothing distracts from the elegant simplicity of the structure.*

ABOVE: *Minimalism does not mean a home without things so much as it means a home without things in view. Here, a storage closet designed to hold glasses and bottles is hidden behind doors that close to become part of the wall. A simple bench and table serve for dining. The table can be reduced in size by springing the drop-down panel, and the bench can be easily moved to another grouping. An arrangement of branches and a round glass vase contrast with the angular elements to wonderful effect.*

ABOVE: *Hiding collectibles behind the doors of this simple, elegant wood piece assures a clean, uncluttered environment. A matching cupboard in the background serves the same purpose. When closed, the doors enable the room to assume a totally serene presence.*

ABOVE: *The clean lines of this wood storage unit with its geometric arrangement of shelves serve as a functional and artistic element displaying vessels of various sizes within easy reach of the dining area. Its placement flush with the back wall assures it will not distract from the simplicity of the home, all the while providing easy access to necessary items.*

CHAPTER TWO
GATHERING ROOMS AND KITCHENS

L ife in the 1990s is busier and more complex than ever before. In many households, both parents work, and children's schedules are filled with school, after-school activities, sometimes jobs, and plenty of homework. There is the strain of learning quickly changing technologies and of juggling the demands of personal responsibilities. Everyone needs more time to keep up and get ahead—but there is also a yearning to spend traditional family time. Part of the philosophy of modernism is the recognition that our homes have to serve us better. Whether one has a traditional family, an extended family, or a family of friends living together, the home needs to provide flexible space in which to gather.

Combining living and dining rooms makes gathering easier, and using furniture in these spaces that is more functional as well as made of practical materials will facilitate different activities. The dining table at mealtime will likely be the project table or game table at other times. A stone or glass table may be too heavy to move unless it's on casters, so lighter-weight wood or metal tables are more desirable. Chairs that can be easily stacked and moved also better serve many purposes.

Manufacturers have begun to provide more and more functional furniture. The marketplace offers sleek, lightweight aluminum tables; woven leather and tubular seating; upholstered chairs on wheels that can be rearranged into different seating groups; and sofas made from add-on, chair-size sections. Buy one, buy several, buy more later when you need them. Dual-function furniture pieces, such as coffee tables that can be raised to become dining tables; side tables with removable tray tops; and cabinets that hide the computer, a file drawer, a printer, and the telephone—the basics for a home office—behind closed doors, reduce the need for several differrent furniture pieces, thus encouraging more spacious design schemes.

Durable, natural materials are both practical and visually appealing. Floors of wood or stone are becoming more popular throughout the home, frequently even being used innovatively in bathrooms.

When kitchens open into living and dining areas, they enable family members to pursue separate tasks and still be together. Busy families have little enough time to cook, do household planning, spend

OPPOSITE: *A floor-to-ceiling window wall juxtaposes the muted, natural colors of brick and stone outside with the solid, vivid colors of the sofa upholstery and the kitchen. Steel beams neatly frame this gathering room while a minimum of furniture supports the modern effort. The geometric, stairlike design of a partial wall serves as both a visual delight and a room divider to the kitchen area.*

time with each other, and chat with friends face to face. Kitchens that offer counters with pull-up stools as part of a cooktop island enable the household chef to perform necessary duties while finding out about a new teacher or the outcome of a soccer practice.

To design a kitchen in modern style presents perhaps the greatest challenge in the home because the kitchen is the hearth, and for many, there is a direct relationship between the amount of visible chinaware and gadgetry and welcomeness. But minimalism provides solutions that make the kitchen not only warm and welcoming, but clutter-free: solid-door cabinets without moldings; unadorned walls; streamlined appliances; and countertops with a minimum of decorative accessories (there may be only one or two functional and artistic items on display). Perhaps there will be a sleek piece of storage furniture close by. True minimalists encourage the reduction of collections: pare down the number of dishes or kitchen accessories—or keep them out of sight.

ABOVE: *An open-plan room with several seating groups offers family members separate interactions, joint conversations, or individual reflection while in proximity to others. Well-chosen accessories add interest, and the warmth of the natural wood floor unites the disparate areas.*

ABOVE: *In this living space, chairs on casters roll easily to the kitchen counter or to the drafting table or easel. Wood floors facilitate movement of furniture. The most important aspect of this space is that it is actually a converted elementary school gymnasium, supporting the recycling ideal of modern style.*

ABOVE: *Antique-style furnishings updated in colorful modern upholstery support the post-modernist desire to make the old new again. An area rug in complementary tones ties the seating area together.*

OPPOSITE: *This sophisticated design scheme has strong art deco overtones, evident in the egg-shaped chairs and dining room torchères. The kitchen is cleverly encapsulated within the confines of the larger space.*

ABOVE: *In this home, modern style meets rustic charm and the results are delightful. The wooden beams and shutters, traditional country elements both, seem perfectly at home, lending their warmth and dignity to the clean, geometrical lines of the room. A farmhouse table, timeless in design, proves that country living and modern style can coexist in harmony.*

BELOW: *In this combined kitchen, dining room, and gathering room, the patterns of the cabinets, countertop, and slate floor complement each other and tie the space together. The back cabinets feature open-shelf storage units, perfect for housing bottles of wine or various pieces of stemware. A rolling cart acts as a bar and can be easily moved to anywhere in the space.*

ABOVE: *Post-modernists applaud converted spaces. This former church is graced with an abundance of natural light from its dramatic arched windows. A mix of old and new furniture lends a casual touch to this grand space without distracting from its architecture.*

ABOVE: *A contemporary design achieves an unusual combination of openness and intimacy with the use of only a partial wall in this loft with very high ceilings. The industrial blue-gray floor and columns are warmed by the natural wood and the sunlight from the various skylights. Huge torchères bathe the scene with soft reflected light at night. The simple table and unique, high-backed chairs make the living/dining space versatile as well as comfortable.*

LEFT: *Sleek and modern, this minimalist-inspired home combines shades of gray with industrial materials like stainless steel and glass. Upper-level windows pour sunlight into the space. A wonderful contrast, polished stone is used for an open hearth while rough-hewn stone lines the wall behind the hearth. A series of streamlined closets designed for the back wall provides the storage so necessary to maintain this simple and affecting space.*

LEFT, TOP: *A wall of windows and a polished bare wood floor provide the perfect backdrop for a set of Windsor chairs around an Eero Saarinen–design table in this eclectically furnished setting. Firewood is neatly organized in a stylish red rolling cart that can easily be moved to each of the home's fireplaces.*

LEFT, BOTTOM: *The serenity nature provides can influence the placement of dining tables. Here, meals can be enjoyed in an all-natural, all-wood setting in front of an enormous window wall, which can be blocked out when the sun is too bright by a simple, natural-toned curtain of fresh linen. Accessories are few. Perhaps the only decoration needed is a vase of long-stemmed vibrant flowers.*

OPPOSITE: *A plate of sandblasted glass that touches neither floor nor ceiling separates this kitchen from the dining area. A less than full wall between the rooms allows light and air to flow freely. Strikingly modern in design, the dining table and chairs dominate the room.*

LEFT: *Natural wood flooring makes for a great base in this partially enclosed outdoor dining area. An abundance of natural light pours in through the open ceiling during the day while track lighting has been installed for nighttime dining. Cast-iron, cushionless chairs feature a symmetrical grid design that is echoed in the tablecloth.*

RIGHT: *This rooftop deck needs little more than a table and chairs for decoration, given the richness of its view. The table is sleek in its construction, made from a plate of glass that rests on an uncomplicated stainless steel frame. The chairs pick up the table frame's design and material, and introduce color to the setting with symmetrically woven backs and seats.*

LEFT: *Modern-style concepts can be incorporated into any style kitchen: even a country kitchen can be minimal in design. Here, simple white beadboard cabinets and a group of drawers with farmhouse pulls contain serving utensils. Glass-doored cabinets, lighted from within to simulate natural light, hold colorful cups and bowls. The wood extension of the sink/work counter with pull-up stools provides a setting easily employed for breakfasts, light dinners, or homework. The white refrigerator helps to maintain the unity of the white design scheme.*

RIGHT: *Utilitarian and beautiful, this kitchen is a minimalist's dream come true, with its clutter-free appearance created through clean white paint and stainless steel. The gray tile floor is the only introduction of color. A sisal mat warms the space.*

BELOW: *Artistic cabinet door and drawer pulls are prominent in this otherwise sleek kitchen. Opaque glass cabinet doors reveal the shapes of dishes behind them, but the shelves and counter have been carefully left uncluttered. The beauty of the natural wood of the cabinets, the texture of the stone backsplash, and the wide-planked wood floors provide a serene corner of natural elements in which to work.*

ABOVE: *Modern kitchens at their most elegant are deceptively simple in design, emphasizing functionality over all. In this narrow, curving kitchen, counter space and storage are abundant. Polished wood cabinets in an appealing hue warm up the space while large windows enable natural light to flood the room.*

OPPOSITE: *Having a place for everything helps keep clutter at bay. The white cabinetry and stainless steel counters provide a serene backdrop for the artistry of the contemporary stone flooring.*

LEFT: *Convenient and stylish, stainless steel is perfect in the kitchen. This true "cook's kitchen" also features natural materials: a granite counter; a central butcherblock preparation surface; and slate tile flooring. The combination is both practical and beautiful.*

ABOVE: *In this streamlined space, elements of design in cabinetry present a dual opportunity: storage and art. Skylights bathe the kitchen in light and glass-paneled doors bring nature into view. A rich butcherblock counter contrasts with a white tile sink surround. The functional stainless steel vent is also a striking art element as its geometric shape echoes the cabinetry glass. It is a minimalist kitchen with maximum appeal.*

ABOVE: *This well-designed kitchen is high on functionality without sacrificing aesthetics. Ample understated storage contains utensils and gadgets, leaving the counter free for a piece of sculpture and an appealing bowl of fruit. Stone counters, warm-toned wood cabinets and drawers, and a long window that provides a garden view and slides open to let in fresh air along with sunlight make this place a pleasurable spot in which to work.*

OPPOSITE: *Open windows and open doors bring the vista of the garden into this clean-lined kitchen and allow natural sunlight to flood the easy-care, built-in counters. Teak storage units contain all kitchen utilities and accouterments. In this uncluttered kitchen a sculptural tea kettle, a delicate lighting pendant, and a classic toaster capture the eye and are the only embellishments needed.*

CHAPTER THREE

BEDROOMS

More than most rooms in the home, the bedroom has a tendency to collect "stuff." Yet, if it is to serve as a sanctuary, the bedroom should be calming, not cluttered. Modern style offers a chance to design the bedroom as a haven, a place from which distracting elements have been banned and serenity reigns.

Start by eliminating anything that does not need to be in the bedroom. For most people, that means keeping the bed, perhaps a nightstand, a place to store clothing, and in many cases, a television.

As the centerpiece of the room, the bed is the most important piece of furniture. It may be minimal—a simple, unadorned frame, with stark white linens—or it may be a custom-designed built-in that incorporates lighting and storage. With such a piece, a bedside table is not necessary.

All other pieces in the bedroom should focus on storage, without which even the most stylish bedroom would be eventually mired in clutter. If the bed does not provide built-in compartments for the storage of extra bedding, or off-season clothing like sweaters in the summer, a simple trunk in the same palette as other crucial furnishings in the room may be employed. Additionally, a television, VCR, and stereo system can be easily concealed behind the doors of an armoire specially picked out to blend with the other furnishings in the bedroom decor.

OPPOSITE: *A platform bed unit offers many other uses besides sleeping in this minimalist bedroom. The headboard/wall hides away the electrical wiring for the bed lamps and contains an out-of-sight work area behind the bed, while effectively obscuring the vanity area from view. Horizontal wood panels, actually closet doors, are an appealing design element. Besides the bed and a small wood corner table, the only other element in the room is a large television set opposite the bed. This thoughtful, sculptural scheme offers an easy, natural design and significant facility.*

ABOVE: *The simple, natural elements of this bedroom—the white cotton bedcover, the wood of the floor and door, the muslin shades—offer a sense of beauty, comfort, and calm and tie the modern style scheme together. An added bonus, this bedroom has doors that lead out onto an expansive terrace. Well-placed potted plants bring the outdoors in.*

OPPOSITE: *Here, a platform bed and surround in maple veneer conceals wiring for bedside lighting as well as provides storage. Unshielded windows enable sunlight to spill into the bedroom and provide an elegant view of greenery. A tall straw basket is a simple, natural touch. The bed surround shields the vanity area, which enjoys its own flood of light through upper windows on the other side of the room.*

BELOW: *A full wall of closets answers all of one's shelf and hanging needs when space is limited and, at the same time, provides the only decorative element for which this room has room.*

LEFT: *This bedroom is decorated in soft brown tones thanks to the use of various woods for walls, floors, and closets, as well as a leather art deco–inspired chair. The muted tones provide a simple environment that offers the inhabitant a sense of serenity. The absence of hardware on the bedroom closets only adds to the simple decor. Pure white bedding enhances the design scheme.*

ABOVE: *The elegance of natural light is magnified by a large white shade, which also serves to conceal the radiator and an unattractive lower view in this small bedroom. When space is limited, a closet with shelves as well as a dowel for hanging clothes is preferable to a freestanding dresser. Wicker chests are also great for storage as well as being decorative. Reading lamps are attached to the wall behind the bed, eliminating the need for bedside tables.*

OPPOSITE: *An attic bedroom has been turned into a modern style delight. Whimsically designed, yet sleek and simple cabinetry provides a wealth of storage. Freestanding as opposed to being built-in, it can be moved to a new locale on a moment's notice. The units have been assembled artfully around a narrow window that looks out to the upper branches of a very tall tree and frames a natural leafy view.*

ABOVE: *The wide window in this simple, uncluttered child's room encourages enjoyment of the peaceful, green vista. Truly minimalist in spirit, the room features few but functional furnishings, which include only a small bed, a wicker dresser, settee, and toy trunk, table and chair set, and play-bassinet. Because these are all made from the same material, they do not distract from the spareness of the room.*

LEFT: *An eclectic mix of old and new brings this minimal bedroom to life. A velvet bergère sits beneath a massive wood-framed oil painting, injecting a sense of history and a welcome punch of color. An assortment of small wooden boxes attests to the owner's enthusiasm for collecting. A simple platform bed sits serenely in the center. The furnishings, though few, imbue the room with personality and flair.*

A B O V E : *In a bedroom with sliding glass doors that open to a terrace and a breathtaking natural spectacle, curtains are needed only to provide privacy. The white crepe curtains in this room do not detract from the wonderful view. A graceful dressing table can double as a desk, lessening the need for excess furniture. The sleek curves of the minimal stainless steel chair nicely complement the curves of the desk.*

ABOVE: *Living room. Home office. Bedroom. This space encompasses many functions while remaining streamlined and sophisticated.*

OPPOSITE: *Tucked in the corner of a bedroom, this small daybed offers a cozy spot for reading. Floor-to-ceiling glass allows sunlight to flood the room while sliding doors open the room to the warm and cool breezes, day and night. The minimalist-inspired fireplace provides the charm of glowing logs as well as warmth, without compromising the strict geometry of the space.*

CHAPTER FOUR
BATHROOMS

In designing a bathroom, the modern goal is to expand the experience of relaxation, renewal, and separation from worldly pressure. The ideal is to use natural materials, to open the room to natural light, and to include adequate hidden storage to allow peaceful surroundings, devoid of the usual vanity clutter.

Enlarging windows will allow for a flood of natural light. Privacy concerns can be met with bottom-up or top-down shades, or sandblasted glass. If windows are at an angle to foliage, mirrors might be positioned effectively to reflect nature's vistas. The use of subdued, natural materials—stone, wood, and slate—can create a serene space by bringing nature's beauty indoors.

A bathroom designed with suitable storage to avoid countertop disarray will be a space that is more visually satisfying. It can be an oasis of calm and pleasure. Elegant and unusual basins and faucets can become artworks in themselves. Even the most minimal style bathroom can provide a home version of a luxury retreat.

When it is not practical to create an entirely new bathroom, smaller changes to an existing space can achieve some of the desired effects. Perhaps a window can be enlarged. A column of narrow storage cabinetry can hide much of the usual clutter, providing a little more breathing room. Changing hardware—sink faucets and bath and shower hoses—can update an old design, while the new glass sink basins add a jewel-like presence.

Given today's busy lifestyle, there seems never to be enough time for oneself. The modern style bathroom/spa, at whatever level you achieve it, can become a private place where the pressures of the outside world can be pushed far away for a few moments, where natural materials and artistic elements come together to facilitate serenity and relaxation.

OPPOSITE: *Truly modern style in spirit, this streamlined bathroom sink area is without clunky or unnecessary "extras." A stainless steel basin sits atop a granite pedestal, which serves to disguise plumbing. A second granite panel contains the faucet and also hides unsightly pipes. A large slatted wood closet contains toiletries or anything that might have been held in a vanity or medicine cabinet.*

ABOVE: *Here, the use of light-colored wood with artistic joinery provides one of the quietly pleasing elements in this carefully designed bathroom. A cobalt blue basin that sits atop the vanity counter is a delightful touch. Ample storage enables a clutter-free space. The elegant lighting enhances the enjoyment of the updated minimalism of this private place.*

ABOVE: *Sliding doors with opaque glass panes provide privacy and disguise the bathroom from the bedroom side. Because the bathroom lacks a window with which to brighten the space with natural light, the color treatment embraces soft natural hues. The warm tone of the marble counter complements the paleness of the bleached oak door frames and undercounter cabinets, providing a light, monochromatic unity.*

OPPOSITE: *The glass wall and all-glass sink provide a clear view of the natural wood deck and pool below and the vista beyond. Here the bathroom/spa is like a hideaway, a place from which to see but not be seen. The vista is the only decoration needed in the almost invisible room.*

ABOVE: *The plate glass wall at the end of the vanity counter opens this inviting bathroom to a long view of grasses and trees. A full-wall mirror behind the sink reflects the view and visually enlarges the space. The matte tone of the stone countertop and the random joining of stone tiles on the floor draw one's focus. A glass ceiling supported by slender wood beams adds more natural light to the space, and the soft color of the wood cabinetry is in elegant contrast to the darker colors. Designed with drawers and doors to shelving that have no knobs or pulls, the cabinetry helps to maintain the purity of the space.*

ABOVE: *Bathing while gazing at the sea invites serenity for mind and body. The hard natural surfaces of this spa are softened by the graceful plants in the container box at the foot of the Jacuzzi tub. Sunlight tempered by protective window film floods this private space. Note the elegant, artistic tap for filling the tub.*

ABOVE: *The character of a small bathroom can be changed dramatically by removing part of a wall and replacing it with a large window. In this case the window not only provides a remarkable vista, but also likely changes the personal perspective while bathing. New fixtures for the shower and sink add artistic elements. Floor-to-ceiling tile visually enlarges the space, while the soft tone of the tile enhances the setting.*

ABOVE: *Light pours into this sea-toned bathroom through a large window behind the bathtub. Additional light comes in through small rectangular windows at the top of the wall, providing a natural source of light for the shower. Frosted glass doors create privacy, while allowing even more light into the shower.*

ABOVE: *The plumbing works are hidden in this provocative design for a bathroom. The exciting pattern created by the two-tone grains of the wood cabinets is calmed by the quiet black stone surfaces of the sink, toilet, and bathtub. The use of rich natural materials imbues this pared-down space with its own strong personality.*

LEFT: *Here, the use of artistic materials and a careful attention to scale achieve an elegant design in a small bathroom. The smoked glass basin seems suspended from the wall, while a slender spigot serves the function of sinktop faucets. A narrow oak closet cleverly conceals towels and assorted toiletries. The focus of this modern style bathroom becomes the materials and the design, not the size.*

OPPOSITE: *In this example of pure minimalism, the repetition of the rectangular shapes—in the floor blocks, the stone tub, and the window—invites contemplation. Soothing and serene with its uninterrupted stone surfaces, this bathroom offers no distraction from its intended purpose. The purity of the bathing space is animated by only one element—the exaggerated design of the handshower.*

ABOVE: *Here, a wood surround on a porcelain tub gives a softer, woodsy feeling to a traditionally hard surface. A large plate-glass window looks out on a view of trees, providing the illusion of bathing outdoors. Panels of wood fit across the top of the tub so that it can be entirely concealed, allowing the surface to be used for other purposes, such as storing towels, when it's not being used for bathing.*

OPPOSITE: *Natural materials such as slate, tumbled marble, and stone form the walls and floor in this ultracontemporary bathroom. A textured paint treatment emulates the look of stone on the walls of the bathing area. Sunlight spills onto the patio open to the sky. The idea of recycling rings true in this space, as an antique clawfoot tub is given new life with the addition of stainless steel "feet."*

ABOVE: *In a private bedroom suite, the bath can be satisfyingly open to the larger space. The style and use of marble and stone here are reminders of luxurious baths from ages past. Bare but for the beauty of the hardware and the stone, the focus is on the experience of the bath.*

CHAPTER FIVE

ELEMENTS OF DESIGN

Good design is in the details. And in a modern or minimalist decor, with so few elements, the details make all the difference. The use of color and texture, the choice of accessories, the placement of furniture—all of these can determine the style of a room.

Where purists once rejected color in favor of all white, today the use of neutral tones—even different shades of a neutral in one room—offers intriguing possibilities without detracting from the serenity of the room. Flashes of more intense color may be employed to draw the eye to a focal point or to transform a room from dull to dramatic.

While minimalists reject excess, their ideas about the number of elements with which to accessorize vary. Where one might fill just the right shaped vase with an arrangement of branches and bar the use of any other accessory, another may feel that more elements are necessary. Collections of accessories may be used to dramatic effect in even the sparest of rooms.

Part of what is interesting about modern style is the flexibility of design. Often, fewer pieces of furniture are used because the pieces used offer dual functions. Mixing styles and periods of furniture is provocative and appealing—the modern room embraces the past without sacrificing the modern aesthetic. A single, well-made piece of furniture, carefully positioned, may define an entire room. Or a collection of different pieces, each chosen for its intrinsic beauty, can make a room special. Experimentation is the essence of modern style.

Ultimately, it is the details that express the room's character. So feel free to experiment with them until your home expresses your own modern style.

OPPOSITE: *East meets West in a knowledgeable mix of curves and straight lines. The palm tree peeking from beyond the Moorish-style arch emphasizes the delicately exotic reference, as does the detailing along the bottom edge of the balcony wall. The discreetly antique Western chair stands like a handsome piece of sculpture on the burnished wood floor. Shades of brown artfully bring the various elements together.*

OPPOSITE: *The provocative color of a concrete patio wall is enlivened by the presence of complementary-colored terra-cotta vases, demonstrating that modern style doesn't necessarily mean "stark" and "white," rather, it means simple, pared-down, and warm.*

ABOVE: *Some forethought went into the design of this courtyard wall, wherein architecture and nature have come together spectacularly in the sunlit pattern formed by the grid of the wall. Painting the wall a vivid color also makes the result an important decorative element.*

ABOVE: *Some chairs are designed to look like art when in use or when stacked. Epitomizing the clean style and convenience of modern style design, these stacking chairs can be easily cleared away when space is needed for another activity, and then just as easily rearranged for seating at mealtimes.*

OPPOSITE: *The intricate base of this small table provides a charming visual accent, and it is easy to move when reconfiguring furniture groups. A simple dish with fruit provides a subtle decoration.*

ABOVE: *A stone, rather than all-brass, doorknob shows a post-modern appreciation for the use of natural materials in even the smallest details in the home.*

LEFT: *A massive hammered aluminum fireplace is large enough to also serve as a room divider between living room and kitchen. It is a strong example of a striking and functional element becoming the primary decorative element.*

OPPOSITE: *A purist might leave this corner empty, feeling that the geometric shape of the wall and the striking way in which it is painted make a sufficient statement. Yet the clean, curvy lines of the rocking chair echo those of the slender pedestal table at its side, an elegant and spare vignette to call attention to the corner.*

RIGHT: *Furniture that can be folded up and tucked away, such as this dining set, is particularly appealing for flexible living and families on the move. That the gleaming polished wood furniture complements the polished wood floor is another bonus.*

ABOVE: *The famous Le Corbusier lounge chair was first manufactured in 1927. It is one of the pieces of furniture in the design collection of New York's Museum of Modern Art. Its sleek design with stainless steel frame and black base and cushion makes it a work of art in this spare, black-and-white setting.*

ABOVE: *A statement about the beauty of natural materials is being made here with an unusual straw chair on a jute rug with a rustic wood side table and windows covered with rice-paper screens.*